FESTIVAL of CAROLS

MUSIC BY JOSEPH M. MARTIN
NARRATION BY PAMELA MARTIN
ORCHESTRATION BY BRANT A

T0079557

CONTENTS:

Performance Time: Approx. 50 minutes

Harold Flammer
M U S I C

A Division of Shawnee Press, Inc.
1107 17th Avenue South • Nashville, TN 37212

Visit Shawnee Press Online at www.shawneepress.com

PERFORMANCE NOTES

This work follows the order of the traditional Lessons and Carols service and includes all nine Scripture lessons. Each lesson has been written in a more contemporary form, while attempting to keep the lyrical flow of the older texts. Churches that wish to substitute the Scripture translation of their choice may, of course, do so.

Traditionally, a small child reads the first lesson. Lay people and staff of increasing rank or roles of responsibility within the church read the subsequent lessons (two through eight), with the minister reading the ninth and final lesson. However, in this interpretation of the service, we suggest readers who might represent the lessons or anthems in some way; for instance, a choir member might read the seventh lesson which describes the choir of angels. The minister gives the opening bidding prayer and the closing blessing/prayer.

Readers may process into the sanctuary with the choir and sit together. Optionally, they may come forward from their individual seats when it is their time to read or (if miked) may stand and read from their place in the sanctuary. Each reader recites the number and title of the lesson, gives the book reference, and reads the scripture lesson. (Italicized Scripture references are for information only and are not to be read aloud.) Remind readers to read slowly and distinctly. After the reading of each lesson, the reader leads the congregation in the response: "Thanks be to God." (Readings and responses may be printed in the Order of Worship.)

The reader of the bidding prayer needs to be in place well before measure 39 of "A Christmas Processional."

Traditionally, the congregation stands for the processional and the bidding prayer. You may either follow this tradition or choose to have the congregation remain seated until measure 109 of "A Christmas Processional," at which time they may stand, join in singing the final stanza of "O Come, All Ye Faithful," and be seated at its conclusion.

Suggested Readers:

If possible, select readers who relate to the examples given in the lesson or in the anthem that follows. Suggested readers:

Bidding Prayer:	minister or celebrant
The First Lesson:	a father
The Second Lesson:	a youth
The Third Lesson:	an elder or deacon
The Fourth Lesson:	a young child
The Fifth Lesson:	a young girl
The Sixth Lesson:	a pregnant woman or young mother
The Seventh Lesson:	a choir member
The Eighth Lesson:	a teacher
The Ninth Lesson:	an acolyte or candle lighter
Closing Prayer and Blessing:	minister or celebrant

Optional visual aids:

If desired, visual symbols may be used to reinforce the readings; these symbols may be placed on the altar. Suggested symbols:

The First Lesson:	a rose or thorns
The Second Lesson:	sand, poured into a dish
The Third Lesson:	a small unlit candle
The Fourth Lesson:	a leafy twig or branch
The Fifth Lesson:	a crown
The Sixth Lesson:	straw
The Seventh Lesson:	a cloth
The Eighth Lesson:	a small, wrapped gift
The Ninth Lesson:	the Christ candle, lighted

Banners:

Many churches use banners during the season of Advent and Christmas. You may wish to bring a banner forward for each lesson or they may be brought in during the opening processional. Suggested banner symbols:

The First Lesson:	a rose with thorns or a tree
The Second Lesson:	many tiny stars
The Third Lesson:	a sun or a candle
The Fourth Lesson:	a lamb and a lion, or a budding branch
The Fifth Lesson:	a dove
The Sixth Lesson:	a manger
The Seventh Lesson:	a shepherd's crook or a lamb
The Eighth Lesson:	one large star or three crowns
The Ninth Lesson:	an open Bible or the Chi Rho symbol

4

*dedicated to Martha Jane and David J. Diehl in thanksgiving for their 40 years of music ministry
to St. Luke's Episcopal Church, Metuchen, New Jersey*

A CHRISTMAS PROCESSIONAL

Arranged by
JOSEPH M. MARTIN (BMI)

A8786

* Tune: IRBY, Henry John Gauntlett (1805-1876)
Words: Cecil Frances Alexander (1818-1895)

A8786

6

A8786

Bidding Prayer:
Let us prepare our

hearts to hear God's Word. Once more, let us hear of His plan to redeem us from darkness by

sending the Light of His Son. Through the reading of the Word may we, like the shepherds,

hear the angels. In our hearts, may we also journey to Bethlehem and see the Child in a manger.

But first we pray for this Church and for those we are called to serve. We ask for hearts of

goodwill in our families and among our neighbors, in our communities and among nations,

* Both repeats are optional and should only be used if extra time is needed for the narration.
A8786

that we might truly have peace on earth. Amen.

SOPRANO

ALTO

TENOR

BASS

*O come,   all   ye   faith - ful,

joy - ful   and   tri - um - phant, O   come____ ye, O

* Tune: ADESTE FIDELES, John Francis Wade (1711-1786)
  Words: John Francis Wade

Sing,___ all ye cit - i - zens of ___ heav - en a-

bove! Glo - ry to God,___ all

glo - ry in the high - est!_____ O

come, let us a - dore Him, O come, let us a -

dore Him, O come, let us a - dore_____ Him,_____

Christ_____ the Lord!

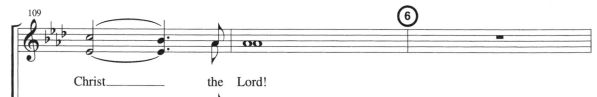

* Part for congregation is included on the enhanced listening CD - ND6016.

morn - ing. Je - sus, to Thee___ be all

morn - ing. Je - sus, to Thee___ be all

glo - ry giv'n. Word of the

glo - ry giv'n. Word of ___ the

READER:

The First Lesson: The fall of Adam
From the Book of Genesis:

Just before twilight, as the evening breeze began to blow, Adam and Eve heard God walking in the garden. Knowing that they were naked, they were afraid and hid from Him among the trees, but God called out to Adam, "Where are you?" And Adam answered, "When I heard you, I hid because I was naked." Then God asked him, "Who told you that you were naked? Have you disobeyed me by eating from the forbidden tree?" Adam replied, "The woman you gave me as a companion, she offered me fruit from the tree, and so I ate it." Then God asked Eve, "What have you done?" and Eve replied, "The snake tricked me into eating the fruit." God turned to the snake and said, "Because you have done this, I will curse you and you will be despised above all living things. For the rest of your days, you will crawl on your stomach and eat the dust of the earth. You and your offspring will be lifelong enemies of the woman and her children. You will bite them on the heel and they will strike you on the head." And to Adam, God said, "Because you disobeyed me, I will curse the dust from which you were made. Only by the sweat of your labor will the ground produce enough food for you to eat. For the rest of your life, you will struggle to make a living out of the dust, and when you die, to that same dust you will return." *(Genesis 3:8-15, 17-19)*

ALL: Thanks be to God.

written to God's glory for the choirs of White Plains United Methodist Church, Cary, NC

A FATHER'S LOVE, A PERFECT ROSE

Arranged by
JOSEPH M. MARTIN (BMI)

* Tune: DIVINUM MYSTERIUM, 13th century Plainsong
Words: Aurelius Clemens Prudentius (348-413), tr. John M. Neale (1818-1866) and Henry W. Baker (1821-1877), alt.

20

He the source, the end - ing, He.

SOPRANO
ALTO
*Lo,____ how a Rose e're bloom -

TENOR
BASS

from ten - der stem____ has sprung!

ing,____ from ten - der stem____ has sprung!

from ten - der stem has sprung!

* Tune: ES IST EIN ROS', *Geistliche Kirchengesäng*, 1599
Words: anonymous, tr. Theodore Baker (1851-1934), alt.

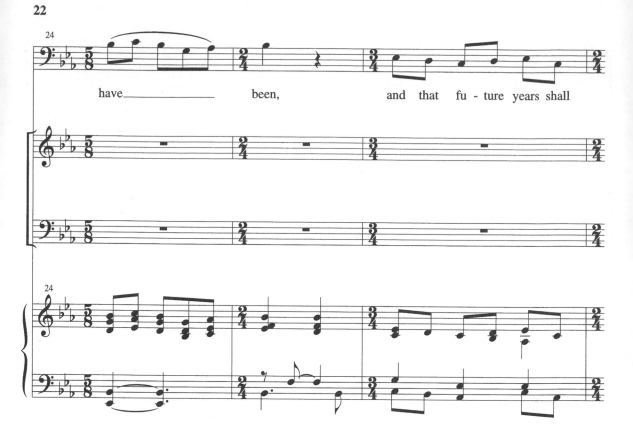

have_____ been,   and that fu - ture years shall

(solo tacet to measure 48)

see,   ev - er - more and ev - er - more!_____

It

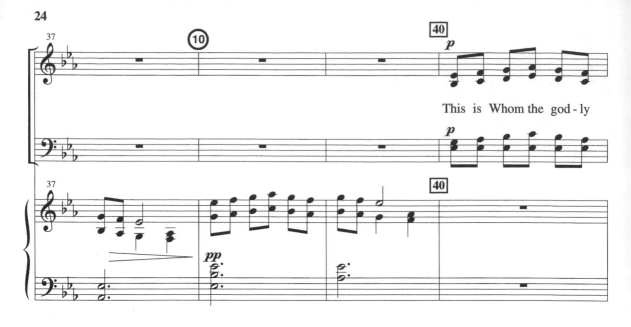

This is Whom the god-ly proph-ets chant-ed of in one___ ac - cord;___

Whom the voic-es of the an - cients___ prom-ised in their faith - ful

BARITONE SOLO (opt. T.B. unison)

I - sai - ah 'twas fore - told it, the word.

Rose I have ___ in mind. With Ma - ry

Oh ___

A8786

we be - held it, the vir - gin moth - er

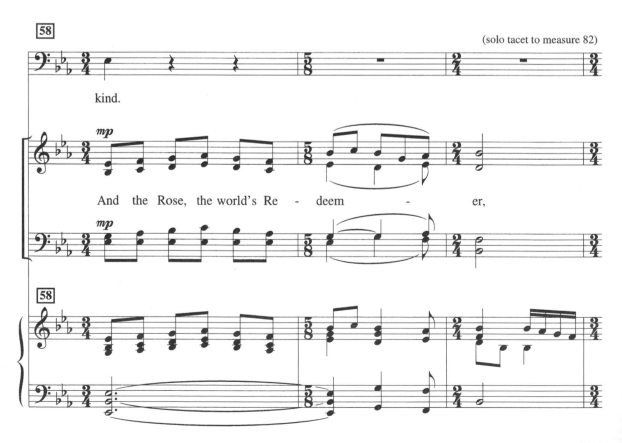

(solo tacet to measure 82)

kind.

And the Rose, the world's Re - deem - er,

A8786

spread the fra - grance of God's grace,_____ ev - er - more,

ev - er - morc, cv - er - more._____

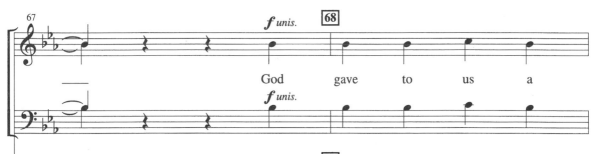

God gave to us a

28

A8786

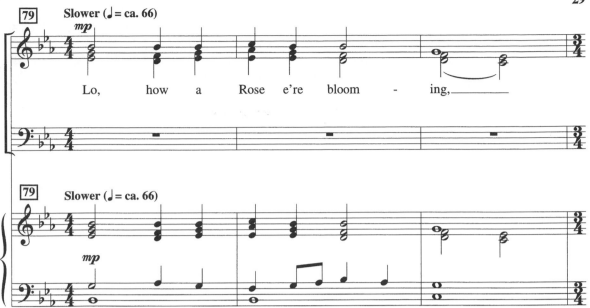

Lo, how a Rose e're bloom - ing,

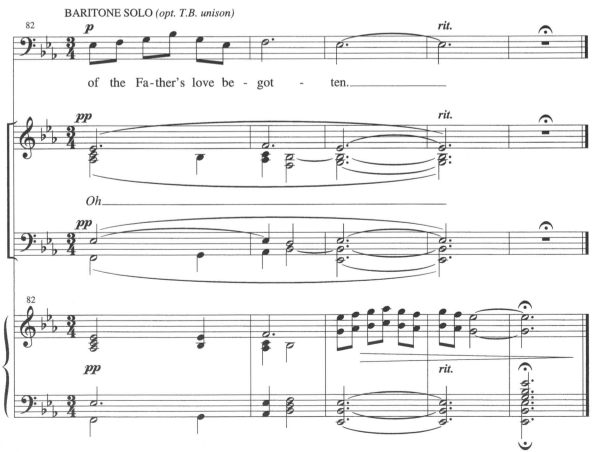

BARITONE SOLO *(opt. T.B. unison)*

of the Fa-ther's love be - got - ten.

Oh

READER:
The Second Lesson: God's covenant with Abraham
From the Book of Genesis:

The angel of the Lord called to Abraham, "Because you have obeyed God and were willing to sacrifice your only Son, the Lord makes this solemn promise: 'Your descendants will outnumber the stars in the heavens and the grains of sand upon the shores. And through you and your children, all nations of the earth will be blessed.'"
(Genesis 22:15-18)

ALL: Thanks be to God.

O COME, O COME, EMMANUEL

Words: anonymous
Translation by
JOHN MASON NEALE (1818-1866)
and HENRY SLOANE COFFIN (1877-1954)

Based on tune:
VENI EMMANUEL
15th Century Plainsong
Arranged by
JOSEPH M. MARTIN (BMI)

(*f*) come, O come, Em - man - u - el, and ran - som cap - tive
(*mf*) come, Thou Day - spring, come_____ and cheer our spir - its by Thine

* Part for congregation is included on the enhanced listening CD - ND6016.

34

READER:
The Third Lesson: The birth of Christ foretold
From the Book of Isaiah:

The people who walk in darkness will see a great Light, a Light that will shine on everyone, even those who live in the shadow of death.

A Child will be born to us, a Son given who will be our leader. We will call Him Wonderful Counselor, Mighty God, Everlasting Father, and Prince of Peace. His kingdom and the peace it brings will last forever and He will rule with justice and goodness. *(Isaiah 9:2, 6-7)*

ALL: Thanks be to God.

CELTIC ADVENT CAROL

Words by
MICHAEL BARRETT
and **JOSEPH M. MARTIN**

Music by
DAVID ANGERMAN (ASCAP)
MICHAEL BARRETT (BMI)
and **JOSEPH M. MARTIN (BMI)**

Published separately: A8683

A8786

40

A8786

Will you be read-y for Him when He comes,_____ When He comes? Light the can-dle, Je-sus is com-ing._ O-pen your hearts, pre-pare ye the way. Sleep-ers a-wake, for

43

A8786

Cap - ti - vum sol - ve Is - ra - el. Ve - ni, Em -
(opt.) Come now and ran - som Is - ra - el.

man - u - el. Je - sus is com - ing. Je - sus is com - ing.

Could He be com - ing to - day?

READER:
The Fourth Lesson: The peace of Christ foretold
From the Book of Isaiah:

From the ancient roots of David's family tree, a shoot will spring up, a new Branch that will bear fruit. This Branch will blossom with the wisdom, power, and understanding that come from obedience to God. He will not be influenced by outward appearance or unreliable testimony, but will exercise fairness over the poor and needy and bring justice to those who break His law.

There will come a day when the wolf and the lamb will live together peacefully, a time when the leopard will sleep next to the goat and the lion beside the deer, and a little child will care for them.

The cow and the bear will eat side-by-side and their young will lie down together. The lion will no longer be a predator, but will eat straw like the ox. Children will play near the snake's den and not be in danger. No creature will harm or be harmed for creation will overflow with the ways of God. *(Isaiah 11:1-3a, 4a, 6-9)*

ALL: Thanks be to God.

49

COME, THOU LONG-EXPECTED JESUS

Words by
CHARLES WESLEY (1707-1788)

Based on tune: **HYFRYDOL**
by ROWLAND H. PRICHARD (1811-1887)
Arranged by
JOSEPH M. MARTIN (BMI)

* Part for congregation is included on the enhanced listening CD - ND6016.

Copyright © 2008 Malcolm Music
(A Division of Shawnee Press, Inc., Nashville, TN 37212)
International Copyright Secured. All Rights Reserved.

A8786

long - ex - pect - ed Je - sus, born___ to___ set Thy___

peo - ple free. From___ our fears___ and sins___ re -

lease___ us. let___ us___ find our___ rest___ in Thee.

joy____ of ev - 'ry long - ing heart.

Born Thy peo - ple to de - liv - er,

54

By   Thine   all_____   suf - fi - cient   mer - it,

raise   us   to_____   Thy   glo - rious   throne!

By_____   Thine   own_____   e - ter - nal   spir - it,

A8786

READER:
The Fifth Lesson: The angel Gabriel's appearance to Mary
From the Gospel According to Luke:

God sent the angel Gabriel to the town of Nazareth with a message for a young girl. The girl's name was Mary and she was engaged to a man named Joseph, a descendant of David. The angel greeted her with these words, "You have been highly regarded by God, and He is with you." As Mary thought about the meaning of this, the angel continued, "Do not be afraid, Mary. God has chosen you to become a mother. You will have a Son and you are to name Him Jesus. He will rise to power and be called the Son of the Highest. God will give Him David's throne and He will rule His people forever." Mary asked the angel, "How can I have a child since I am a virgin?" And the angel said, "This will happen by the power of the Lord. His Spirit will be upon you, for this child will be the Son of God Himself." At this, Mary said, "I am willing to serve God as He sees fit; let it be as you have said." Then the angel Gabriel left. *(Luke 1:26-35, 38)*

ALL: Thanks be to God.

MY SOUL DOTH MAGNIFY THE LORD

Words by
JOSEPH M. MARTIN

Arranged by
JOSEPH M. MARTIN (BMI)

* Tune: DIVINUM MYSTERIUM, 13th century Plainsong

A8786

58

by the Ho - ly Ghost con - ceiv - ing,____ held the Sav - ior of ____ our

race.

Somewhat faster, with simple joy (♩ = ca. 72)

(choir tacet)

Somewhat faster, with simple joy (♩ = ca. 72)

FEMALE SOLO *(opt. S.A. unison)*

My soul doth mag - ni - fy the

* Tune: WEXFORD CAROL, traditional Irish tune.

A8786

29
(solo tacet)
Light, the Prince of Peace, the prom-ised Christ.
32
26
35
SOPRANO
ALTO
TENOR
BASS
36
p
My soul doth mag - ni - fy the Lord. My soul re -

62

A8786

With all our hearts, God's___love pro - claim and mag - ni

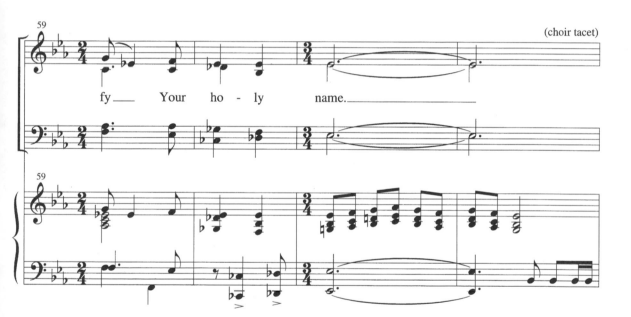

fy__ Your ho - ly name._____

(choir tacet)

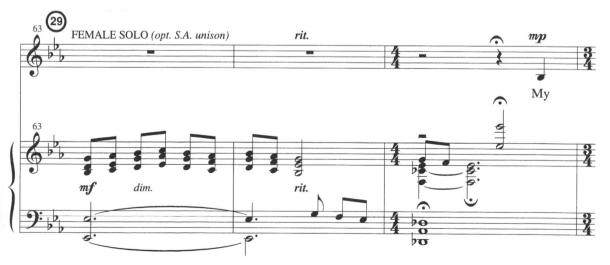

FEMALE SOLO *(opt. S.A. unison)*   *rit.*   *mp*

My

A8786

64

A8786

READER:
The Sixth Lesson: The birth of Jesus
From the Gospel According to Luke:

Soon after this event, the emperor Augustus ordered that a census be taken of his empire. Everyone had to travel to the city of his ancestors to be counted. Since Joseph was a descendant of David, he had to be counted in David's hometown, which was Bethlehem. So he and Mary traveled from Nazareth to Bethlehem. The city was overflowing with visitors and lodging was scarce. While they were there, Mary gave birth to her first Child, a Son. And because the only room available to them was a stable, his cradle was a manger, which was a feeding crib for the animals. *(Luke 2:1, 3-7)*

ALL: Thanks be to God.

CRADLE CAROLS

Arranged by
JOSEPH M. MARTIN (BMI)

CHOIR *and* CONGREGATION *or* CHILDREN'S CHOIR *

** A - way in a man - ger, no crib for a
near me, Lord Je - sus, I ask Thee to

bed, the lit - tle Lord Je - sus lay down His sweet
stay close by me for - ev - er, and love me, I

* Part for congregation is included on the enhanced listening CD - ND6016.
** Tune: MUELLER, James R. Murray, 1841-1905
Words: St. 1, anonymous; st. 2, John Thomas McFarland, 1851-1913

A8786

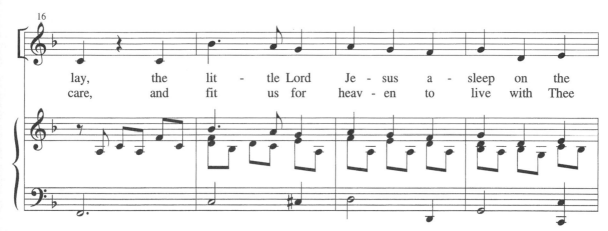

68

* Part for congregation is included on the enhanced listening CD - ND6016.
** Tune: ST. LOUIS, Lewis H. Redner, 1831-1908
   Words: Phillips Brooks, 1835-1893

A8786

* Part for congregation is included on the enhanced listening CD - ND6016.
** Tune: STILLE NACHT, Franz Gruber, 1787-1863
   Words: Joseph Mohr, 1792-1848; tr, John Freeman Young, 1820-1885
A8786

70

A8786

READER:
The Seventh Lesson: The shepherds' journey to the manger
From the Gospel According to Luke:

That night in the hills surrounding Bethlehem, shepherds tended their sheep. An angel of the Lord came to them and a bright light surrounded them. They were terrified, but the angel said to them, "Do not be afraid. I am not here to harm you, but to bring you good news, news of joy for the entire world. A Child has been born in Bethlehem tonight, a Child who will be a Savior to you, who is the Messiah. This is how you will know Him: you will find Him wrapped in cloth, sleeping in a manger." Suddenly many more angels appeared and they praised God, singing, "Glory to God in the highest part of heaven! Peace to all on earth who find favor with Him!" When the angels left, the shepherds said to each other, "Let us go to Bethlehem and see this Child." And they found Mary and Joseph, and the Baby lying in a manger, just as the angel said. *(Luke 2:8-16)*

ALL: Thanks be to God.

A NOEL CELEBRATION

Words by
JOSEPH M. MARTIN

Arranged by
JOSEPH M. MARTIN (BMI)

* Traditional Catalonian Melody

A8786

74

shout with voic - es strong in an ev - er - last - ing song, for this day the world re - joic - es.

Give your praise and lift your voic - es.

Sing No - el!

* Music: Traditional German Melody
  Words: Traditional German Carol, *alt.*

A8786

Come, ye thank-ful

peo - ple come, play the pipe and beat the drum. Tell the

Music: Traditional French Melody
A8786

De - o,　　De - o!

De -　　　　o!

SOPRANO DESCANT *(optional children)*

Sing　to　the Lord.　Sing　to　the Lord.　Sing　to　the Lord.　Sing　to　the Lord.

READER:
The Eighth Lesson: The scholars' pilgrimage to the Child
From the Gospel According to Matthew:

After Jesus was born, a group of scholars traveled from the East to Jerusalem. "Where can we find the One who has been born King of the Jews?" they asked. "A star in the Eastern skies announced His birth and we have followed it so that we might worship Him." When Herod, who was king, heard this, he was alarmed. He brought the chief priests and religious teachers together and asked them, "Where do the Scriptures say that the Messiah will be born?" They answered that the prophet Micah foretold that this would take place in Bethlehem. When he heard this, Herod asked the Eastern scholars when they first saw the star. Then he sent them to Bethlehem saying, "When you have found this new King, let me know so that I may also go and worship Him." So the scholars continued their pilgrimage, following the star. When it stopped over the place where the Child was, they were overjoyed. They entered the house and saw the Child with His mother, and they kneeled before Him, offering gifts of gold, frankincense and myrrh. But having been warned in a dream not to report back to Herod, they returned home by a different way. *(Matthew 2:1-12)*

ALL: Thanks be to God.

A CHRISTMAS INVITATON

Words by
JOSEPH M. MARTIN

Arranged by
JOSEPH M. MARTIN (BMI)

* Tune: KINGS OF ORIENT, John Henry Hopkins, Jr., 1820-1891
Words: John Henry Hopkins, Jr.

*Come ye faith - ful, one and all, to hear the an - gels

* Tune: WASSAIL SONG, Traditional English Tune

88

glo - ry of the Lord! Come and see all the glo - ry of the

Lord! Come and walk be -

neath the star that beams to show the way,

A8786

90

* Tune: SUSSEX CAROL, Traditional English Tune

A8786

God has sent the Prom - ised Son.

A - rise and shine! Your

Light has come. De - clare the works that the Lord has done.

Sing, shout, be ju - bi - lant, all the earth.

Tune: IN DULCI JUBILO, Traditional German Tune
Words: Medieval Latin Carol, 14th century; tr. John Mason Neale, 1818-1866, alt.

A8786

heart and soul and voice. Give ye heed to what we say: Je - sus Christ is born to - day. Christ has o - pened heav - ens door, and we are blessed for - ev - er - more.

READER:
The Ninth Lesson: The mystery of the Incarnation
From the Gospel According to John:

In the very beginning, the One called the Word existed. This Word was with God, and the Word was God Himself. In the beginning the Word and God were one. Through Him everything came into being; nothing came into being without Him. In Him was Life and He gave life to everything He made. His life was like a Light shining in the darkness of human existence. But the darkness was so heavy that people were unable to see the Light, even though it continued to shine despite the darkness.

So God sent a man named John to tell people about the Light, that they might know about it and believe in it. John was not the Light himself; he was sent to announce the Light. The one perfect Light, that gives its light to everyone, was coming into the world. When He came to the world, a world He Himself had made, it did not recognize Him. He came to His own people, the ones He made, and was not welcomed by them. But those who did welcome Him into their lives became children of God like Him. Even though they were not God's flesh-and-blood children, He welcomed them into His family. But Christ, who was the Word, became flesh and blood like us and lived with us. We saw His Light, the Light of the Father shining through the Son, showing us His grace and truth. *(John 1:1-14)*

ALL: Thanks be to God.

A CHRISTMAS THANKSGIVING

Words and music by
JOSEPH M. MARTIN (BMI)

Tune: CRADLE SONG, William J. Kirkpatrick (1838-1921)

A8786

98

A8786

100

A8786

PRAYER AND BLESSING

Congregation stands and remains standing.

Prayer:
Almighty God, as we have heard the reading of Your Word, we remember and give thanks. Remembering that You sent Light into our world, we give thanks that we never need to live in darkness. Remembering that You sent Your Son as one of us, we give thanks that through Him we have become Your children. Remembering Your great love and mercy, with the angels we too give thanks and praise. Amen.

Blessing:
And now, may the Light of the Word shine upon your path and guide
    your way.
May the Light watch over you and be a companion to you by night.
May the Light burn in your hearts and shine through your lives by day.
And through your living, may you be a witness of that Light to the
    world.

A CHRISTMAS RECESSIONAL

Arranged by
JOSEPH M. MARTIN (BMI)

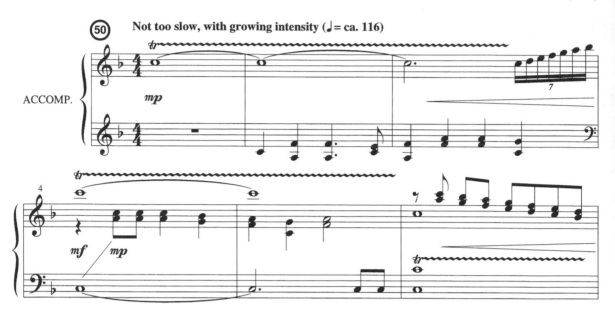

A8786

* Tune: GLORIA, Traditional French Carol
  Words: Traditional French Carol

A8786

in ex - cel - sis De - o!

Glo - - -

- ri - a___ in ex - cel - sis De -

108

* Tune: REGENT SQUARE: Henry T. Smart, 1813-1879
  Words: James Montgomery, 1771-1854

A8786

110

* Hark! the her - ald an - gels sing,___

* Tune: MENDELSSOHN, Felix Mendelssohn, 1809-1847
   Words: Charles Wesley, 1707-1788

112

A8786

With power and majesty (♩= ca. 104)

CHOIR *and* CONGREGATION *

Hail the heav'n born Prince of Peace.___ Hail the Sun of

* Part for Congregation is included in the enhanced listening CD - ND6016.

A8786

116

A8786